Yankee Doodle ★

RIDES AGAIN

Al Hartley

Yankee Doodle galloped into our hearts early in our history and became the symbol of a special kind of freedom.

He still lifts our spirits, reminding us of the adventure and excitement in being free to learn and grow. This is a story rich in fun and action that makes us feel good about our heritage. It encourages us to dream our dreams in a land where they really can come true.

We're free!

MULTNOMAH

Hoofbeats pounded!
Drumbeats sounded!
Heartbeats mounted!
Cannons rolled!

The Redcoats were in control but
they couldn't hold Yankee Doodle.
He knew how to be free!

These were exciting times!
They were "times
    that tried men's souls."
But one man had quit trying.
He'd thrown in the towel
    —the *crying* towel!

Yankee Doodle saw him
and pulled hard on the reins.
"Why are you crying, friend?"
The man sobbed,
    "I'm the town crier!"

"Yes, I see you cry very well.
But aren't you supposed to report
the *news* every night?"

"That's just it," the town crier
sobbed some more. "The news is *bad!*
It's all gloomsday and doomsday!"

"Get hold of yourself," Yankee Doodle
replied. "It's not *all* bad. Maybe
it's just the way you look at it."

And then, with a sob
heard round the world,
the town crier gasped,
"Well *you* look at it! Look
at all those Redcoats!
Look at their man o' wars!
Their cannons! That's *power*!
We'll never win our freedom
against that! And *that's bad news*!"

Yankee Doodle smiled and said
"But there's *good news*, too.
Power isn't only found in military might.
There's power in that church! We're having
a town meeting there to celebrate the
Declaration of Independence!"[1]

"Humph!" the town crier snorted. "You can *declare* independence all you want, but you'll never win it!"

"Have you heard of David and Goliath?"[2] Yankee Doodle asked.

The town crier cried, "That's an old, old story! Face it, Doodle Boy! This is 1776!"

Suddenly,
Redcoat hands
pulled
Yankee Doodle
into the
bushes!

There was lots of
yelling and screaming!
And then—

out came Yankee Doodle

You see,
the Redcoats knew
all about wrestling
on mats in a gym,
but they'd never
tried to wrestle in
a sticker bush
before!

Yankee Doodle
had no trouble
getting free.
He jumped on a
Redcoat cannon
and rode it faster
and faster down
Bunker Hill!

At that very moment, in Redcoat headquarters, the general looked sort of like his teapot: boiling over and ready to blow his top!

"Harumph," he began. "Yankee Doodle is a thorn in our side!

"We must find him!"

Actually, Yankee Doodle
was more than a thorn
in the side of the Redcoats!

He was a loose cannon
busting into their meeting!

The Redcoats
were speechless!

Yankee Doodle
broke the silence
by shouting,
"All in favor of my
motion say, 'Aye'!"

And at that moment
the teapot exploded!

Then the
general exploded,
*"That's him!
Catch him!"*

The Redcoats
flew out the door
as fast as
cannonballs!

This time
they were certain
they had him!

But Yankee Doodle fired the cannon into a huge stack of barrels!

The barrels started to fall, and the Redcoats started to run!

While the Redcoats were busy dodging bouncing barrels, Yankee Doodle heard the church bells announce the town meeting.

He knew everyone who loved freedom would be there!

A young man spoke up!
"I want to go to sea, but
the Lobstercoats stop
our ships and kidnap
our sailors!
There's not even freedom
on the high seas!"

"The Redcoats forced my family
to take soldiers into our home!
They took over my room!
We have to feed them!

"All my friends have Redcoats
in their homes, too!"

"We had a shop and were doing very well, but the Redcoats closed us up tighter than one of their drums!

'We lost our life's savings!"

"We can't let these foreign hands steal the 'life, liberty, and pursuit of happiness' we seek!"[5]

"Our struggle for freedom will continue!"

A young boy rushed into the church with special news:

"The food wagon is ready for General Washington!"

As Yankee Doodle
drove off to
Washington's encampment,
other patriots
lifted the town crier
aboard and laughed,
"Here's another head
of cabbage!"

"This is madness!" the
town crier complained.
"One food wagon for
an entire army?"

The town crier continued
to find bad news everywhere!

"Humph," he grunted,
"what a pitiful army!"

"If your troops keep deserting,
this load of food will be more
than enough! Besides, we
should have brought *shoes* and
firewood for these ragamuffins!"

The words
carried far on the cold wind,
and the patriots felt sorry for
a man who had no hope.

And then the town crier
thought he'd found a real scoop!
"Look at your general!
Driven to his knees!
What a sign of weakness!"

Yankee Doodle simply
said, "Our leader is
praying to the one
who holds our future!"

General Washington
rose and said, "Pass the word!
We cross the Delaware tonight!"

The town crier was
flabbergasted!

"B-but it's Christmas eve!!!"

"Yes," General
Washington said,
"and our scouts
report the Redcoats
are having a party!
We're going to
join them!"

Thus, on December 25, 1776
General Washington gave more orders:
"Leave our campfires burning!
Muffle the cannon wheels!
This will be a surprise party!"

Yankee Doodle knew they were outnumbered,
but he also knew that freedom and
victory were found in the One whose
birthday we celebrate at Christmastime!

And at that moment, across the river,
the Redcoats thought their Christmas
celebration was all fun and games!

In fact, the Redcoats
were having so much fun,
they forgot their duty!

So the patriots joined
in the fun and decided
to make a snowman
with them!

And then the patriots had all the fun!

When Washington's troops finished the snowman, the Redcoats realized the party was over!

Soon, another tempest
in a teapot was brewing
at Redcoat headquarters!
The general's aide disturbed his
sleep with the urgent news,
"Sir, sir, General Washington
is in Trenton!"

"Bully, chaps!"
the general chuckled.
"We've finally captured the sly fox!"

"Sorry, sir,"
an aide choked,
"*He* captured *us!*
He smashed us in Trenton!

He clobbered us in Princeton!
And—gasp—he made off
with our supplies!"

And the Redcoat
general felt as
though his teapot
had flipped its lid
again!

Naturally,
the town crier
was still doing
his thing!

"Okay, so you've
won a few battles!
There's lots of
battles ahead!
There's no way
you'll win the
main event!"

Washington answered
with amazing patience:

"Life's biggest battles
aren't won on the
battlefield! They take
place in our hearts!
Those battles have
names like *fear* and
doubt and *unbelief*!
And you seem to be
losing them, my friend!"

The next five years required strong hearts
because there were many heartbreaks.
Battle after battle was lost.
Folks suffered and sacrificed.

Many of the signers of the Declaration of
Independence were imprisoned and killed![6]

Most saw their homes destroyed,
and all they owned taken by the Redcoats.
But their losses didn't stop them!

They knew that the most valuable thing
in the world is freedom.
And they would leave freedom,
not slavery, for their children!

And then, as the leaves fell one day in the fall of 1781, a scout carried exciting news:

"Cornwallis has grouped his army on the Yorktown peninsula!"

General Washington knew an answer to prayer when he saw one.

"Prepare to march! We can trap the Redcoats!"

"Hold it!" the town crier demanded! "Yorktown isn't around the corner, you know! It's a two-week march! I'm not slogging through all that mud to see your dream of freedom die!"

Yankee Doodle smiled. "Our dream will live as long as we dare to believe!"

And at that moment, a little ray of light entered the town crier's dark world.

Surely, the world had never
seen this breed before!

Patrick Henry spoke for
all patriots when he said,

"Is life so dear, or peace so sweet,
to be purchased
at the price of slavery?
Forbid it, almighty God!
I know not what course
others may take, but as for me,
give me liberty,
or give me death!"[7]

The town crier scratched
his head in amazement!

"Where do these folks get
their spirit? What's the source?"

"Just turn,"
Yankee Doodle said,
"you'll find it!"

Just then the church bells
began to ring as the patriots
marched in faith of victory!

The town crier listened
to the bells and asked
himself, "Are they really
proclaiming liberty?
Can *every* heart really
be set free?"

He entered the church and reached for a Bible.

the one who se
me, and he is
Truth. They sti
didn't underst
that he was tal
bout God
Jesus s
you ha
then

JOHN 8
32 and you will know
the truth and the
truth will set you
free

we are
of Abra
been

He was still puzzled. "What is truth? Where do I find it?" And then he came to the answer. Jesus said, "I am the truth."

Now the town crier understood why the churches of the land had led the struggle for independence

He dropped to his knees and shed a new kind of tear. The old kind had passed away! He found himself praying for those folks of faith who were giving their lives, their fortunes, and their sacred honor for freedom's sake.